DEVELOPING THE CHURCH DRAMA MINISTRY

The Lillenas Drama Topic Series

DEVELOPING THE CHURCH DRAMA MINISTRY

by Paul M. Miller
Author of *Dinner Theatre: Entertaining Outreach*

Lillenas PUBLISHING COMPANY

KANSAS CITY, MO 64141

Cover art: Paul Franitza

Printed in the United States of America

Dedicated to

Martha Bolton, Stephen Hicks and Jerry Cohagan,
Paul McCusker, and Larry Enscoe.
Premier Lillenas playwrights
whose works comprised the first
Lillenas drama catalog.

CONTENTS

PREFACE

The Church Is Ready for Drama Ministry

Some of us alive today can remember when the term *theatre* was a questionable seven-letter word that many born-again Christians did not use, much less frequent.

It was into that kind of world I moved when I discovered that a high school student could have a personal relationship with God, through His Son. For months the wonder of "all things becoming new" outweighed any self-denial—like theatre. Then a question arose: what about the special abilities I seem to have? Drama teachers called them talents; the church I'd forsaken called them gifts.

Right about then, before real depression set in, an alert pastor saw and understood my upheaval. So one evening after a high school rehearsal of *All My Sons*, he met me at the neighborhood soda fountain (very fiftyish), where I was able to express my frustration. Today I credit the Holy Spirit for giving Pastor Sutton insight to what made me tick. He acknowledged that God gives gifts like the ability to express original ideas on paper, as well as interpret other people's ideas on a stage.

While never giving me permission to become a "worshiper of the silver screen" (that's not an original phrase; it's the title of a lurid booklet given to young people like me as a deterrent to life in the theatre), I was wisely encouraged to develop my creative gifts by throwing myself into writing and "putting on skits" for the church's youth society. And did I ever!

Almost every Sunday evening from 6:30 to 7:30, during the denominational Young People's Society hour, the church's other teenager and I presented original dramas that I had written, designed, and rehearsed all Sunday afternoon.

Attendance at our weekly youth meeting became the social event of the church calendar. Our audiences were as diverse as grandmothers from the older ladies' Bible class and giggly kids who lined the two front pews in delicious anticipation for another "show" by Miller and Company.

That *show* began with a dimming of the house lights—accomplished by Mr. Penner, our church custodian, clicking the switches at the back of the sanctuary. This was the cue for footlights—a gooseneck lamp that usually perched on the piano was plugged in and glowed magically on the tired monk's cloth drapes that hung on wooden curtain rings from a wire stretched from one side of the platform to the other. (These drapes gave the older ladies' Bible class privacy during their weekly lesson.)

After a loudly spoken cue to two primary girls, the old curtains swished open and the production began. Incidentally, the position of curtain puller was a highly coveted craft in our "theatre."

The plays? There were so many it is difficult to single out any one as my favorite. However, two immediately come to mind. "My Son, My Son" was presented either at Christmas or Easter; I tend to think it was the latter. In it, Alberta Penner played the role of Mary. All I can recall are two rather dramatic scenes: Mary looking down into the manger with its Shechinah-light bulb, uttering the phrase, "My Son, my Son," followed sometime later by Mary kneeling toward the audience repeating those same lines. Alberta's performance was stellar. She was a first-class trouper and friend. I well remember, in those precontacts days, Alberta tried to go without her glasses, but we had to scrub the idea when she kept running into the scenery.

Probably no Sunday evening production ever equaled Delores Flockhart and my bold venture into eschatology, with an epic show about UFOs, namely flying saucers—which, according to an evangelist we'd just had, were a sure sign of Jesus' soon return. For that presentation, we'd made the skyline of Oakland, Calif., out of cardboard boxes, with little cutout windows that let light bulbs shine through. I'll never forget the audience's reaction when the curtains opened and our set was revealed. There was an audible gasp and, I think, a smattering of applause. (By this time our congregation was becoming theatre-smart.)

The real moment of truth came when paper-plate flying saucers sailed across the stage on a wire we'd stretched over the city, from one side to the other. Each saucer bore a scripture reference for some end-time event like the Jews returning to Israel, World War II, President Roosevelt ("undoubtedly the Antichrist"), the atom bomb, and surely the most convincing, fiery objects in the sky. Ours were placed there by Delores, who was teetering in the wings on a dilapidated step ladder pilfered from Mr. Penner's closet.

If I remember correctly, the production lasted all of 6 minutes; so with 54 more to go, I stepped forward and asked for testimonies and suggested the singing of such then-popular choruses as "Do Lord" and "Safe Am I."

And the Moral of This Story Is . . .

Please understand, in no way am I demeaning those long-ago days in a small Nazarene church on the wrong side of East 14th Street in East Oakland. To the contrary, I'm holding up those wonderful experiences as something good and productive. I believe that God has used them to instill a vision for drama ministries and Lillenas Drama Resources.

It is hoped that this book will give you the courage and commitment to begin or reinstate an organized drama ministry in your church.

Paul M. Miller
Kansas City, Mo.

1.

RECOGNIZE THE BENEFITS OF MEETING BETWEEN PRODUCTIONS

The letters column in *Lillenas Drama Newsletter* often receives observations and questions like this: *I am convinced that drama has great communicative potential for the church. We have just had wonderful success with a production of Paul McCusker's play* Snapshots and Portraits. *A number of folks from the community attended. Many were in our church for the first time. The cast and those who helped learned a lot by trial and error, as well as from the helps in the script book. Here is my question: How can we build on what we have learned, and not start over again with our next play?*

The same basic question has been asked dozens of times in drama conferences and clinics. By this inquiry, the questioner usually means, "Look, I have a hardworking group of actors and tech people who want to keep on learning about their craft. How can we so organize that we will not keep 'reinventing the wheel' with each new production? Also, I want to see our participants grow in their newly found skills."

Another question that relates to the first comes up often from church drama leaders who must prepare a presermon sketch every Sunday. Those letters often read: *In our attempt to be sensitive to the unchurched in our Sunday morning congregation [sometimes Sunday evening] we introduce the sermon theme with a five- to eight-minute worship sketch. Most of the scripts call for two to four participants. To keep from using the same actors every week, we need to establish a talent pool. How can we do this?*

The answer for both of the above situations is generally the same. Whether you are involved in an every-week production schedule or producing plays and sketches on occasion, I encourage you to consider bringing the group together on a regular basis between productions.

Another page from my personal experience journal: For too long our First Drama Ensemble was staging one or two seasons of dinner theatre a year, mounting Christmas and Easter productions, presenting an occasional Sunday evening play or sketch, and throwing together other efforts for better or for worse. Though our major productions were invariably "for better," there were always those lesser times when I wished we'd have had more rehearsal, training, and a better cast.

During these times I would promise myself to get our pool of talent organized. But no one had enough time to schedule more meetings, so, I'd tuck the thought away, only to pull it out again after another performance.

Then a flash of inspiration crashed through. Why not get permission to conduct a drama ministry meeting every week at a time when folks were coming to church anyway? For us that was Wednesday evening, a time when the church has activities for the whole family—Bible study, prayer, choir practice, teen meetings, and kids' programs.

So, with the pastor's blessing, adult drama was added to the Wednesday evening lineup of ministry opportunities. (Teen drama meets from 5:30 to 7:00 each Wednesday evening.)

How often does your group need to get together when there is no play in rehearsal? That will probably depend upon personal calendars and your vision for activity, not to mention the church schedule. For the sake of continuity and momentum, it is difficult to imagine meeting less than once a week.

Points for Organizing

1. Pull together a small group of supporters and brainstorm schedule, activities, and reason for existence. Prepare a mission or purpose statement and a set of guidelines to share with the church leadership. More about this in chapter 3.

2. With a written proposal, based on your discussion, make a presentation to your pastoral staff. You will want to underscore your interest in the ministry, and prove that it will be at the heart of the program. (See chapter 2.) In your written proposal spell out when you want to meet, what you will need as a room, how you plan to keep from competing with other church programs that may be meeting at the same time (like the choir), and so on. If you detect any hesitancy, don't push for a decision in the meeting. In all probability the church board will need to share in the decision.

3. Determine if your drama organization is going to be open to friends from other churches and organizations or limited to yours. Early in our history, we came to the decision that our primary responsibility was to our own constituents. That is, we generally have more auditioneers than we can use from our own church. One the other side of the coin, we have First Drama Ensemblers who came to First Church and became regular attenders because of the drama ministry.

4. Use existing channels of communication to tell the church body what your plans are.

    a. Run a series of interest creators in the Sunday worship folder or midweek newsletter.

    b. Prepare a flyer that can be distributed through Sunday School classes to would-be enthusiasts. Perhaps you ought to include an application for the interested.

    c. Set up an information booth in a high traffic area and distribute the flyer described above. Display some photos from past productions.

5. Draw up your calendar of events and meeting themes and make them available in initial promotion. Probably the flyer mentioned above. (See chapter 4.) It is surprising how many people will take you seriously when they realize that you are organized and have a definite program in the works. In describing that program, make sure you emphasize the following:

    a. The group is open to all who want to be part of a drama ministry. Experience and talents are not a consideration.

    b. Let it be known who is invited to your meetings: teens and adults, teens only, adults only, young adults, seniors, everyone and anyone. This needs to be spelled out with diplomacy. My group is for adults. We invite teens and children to audition for plays that require those ages. There is a group of older adults (my age) who would love to be part of our drama ministry, but they are not comfortable attending the meetings. Some have auditioned on occasion. Teens and children need their own drama program. There is a sample audition sheet in Appendix C.

    c. If you are scheduled to meet during a time when other organizations are meeting, such as the choir, emphasize that folks involved in those ministries are welcome to indicate their interest in drama ministry, and feel free to come to auditions even if unable to be part of the weekly meeting. Be sure to keep these folks aware of what you are doing. I give them a copy of any announcements and the weekly handout when I see them in church the next Sunday.

  6. Include a brief Interest Indicator with your initial announcements. Keep it to the point. Something like this:

Drama Ministry Interest Indicator

YES, by all means count me in for the "get-acquainted" meeting of the the First Church weekly drama ministry group. I understand that the gathering on Thursday night, September 6, at 7:00 in Fellowship Hall doesn't commit me to involvement.

Name _____ Home phone _____

Address _____

Name and address of someone else who might be interested:

_____

_____

Please give or mail this to

[Name]

[Address]

MAKE MINISTRY YOUR REASON FOR EXISTENCE

When word gets out that you are organizing and have a calendar of training meetings and enrichment activities, there should be a wave of interest among folks who have never indicated an interest in your drama group before—at least, that's the way it happened with us.

As mentioned in the first consideration, when you present the organization proposal to the pastoral staff, be sure to underscore ministry—not as window dressing in order to sell the program, but as the principal reason for such an organization's existence.

"Why?" you ask.

Why what?

"Why hype the ministry angle. Can't a church drama program be a drama program without trying to make it legit by tacking on the word *ministry?*"

Do you think that's what we're doing?

"What else should I think? Besides, I don't enjoy schlocky theatre, even at church."

Touché! Schlock and ministry are not synonymous. A slipshod church drama performance cannot be excused because it is for "ministry," any more than believing that sincerity excuses bad singing.

"So, then, how does *ministry* make a positive contribution?"

Good question. Read on.

Whence Ministry?

Back in the early days of our drama group's history, our pastor stopped by the rehearsal room to have a few words with us. His words were something like this.

"I just want you to remember that this group of people is part of the Body of Christ. Everyone who is in that body is involved in a ministry." He opened his New Testament and read these words from Romans 12: "'We have different gifts, according to the grace given us. If a man's [or woman's] gift is prophesying, let him use it in proportion to his faith. If it is serving, let him serve; if it is teaching, let him teach; if it is encouraging, let him encourage; if it is contributing to the needs of others, let him give generously . . .'" (vv. 6-8, NIV).

I looked around at the group as the pastor read. In our room were some highly talented people, some who had lots of experience in high school and college theatre. To them a church drama project like ours allowed them to fulfill some deep personal needs. Sitting in our circle was Sandy, who wonderfully illustrates one phase of our ministry.

Example No. 1: Sandy

Sandy is the mother of twin girls who are ready to graduate from high school. Thirteen years ago she visited First Church as a single mother who had just divorced an abusive husband. When auditions for a church dinner theatre project were announced, Sandy took note, and sure enough, she was present for the reading.

"You're wonderful," I exclaimed, marveling at her voice and interpretation. "Do I detect a bit of Gaelic in your speech?"

"I lived three years in Ireland," she responded. "That's where the girls were born. Their father is an Irishman. While I was there, I performed in community theatre."

The role of the young girl in *The Valiant* was a natural for Sandy. Now, 13 or so years later, she is a pillar of our drama group and of the church. Her daughters are about to become college coeds, and at least one of them is planning on entering some phase of ministry.

Ministry? You bet your life!

Meanwhile, back with the pastor visiting our drama group.

"Let me read one thing more," Pastor added. "It is found in Ephesians 4:11-12: 'He gave some to be apostles, some to be prophets, some to be evangelists . . . pastors and teachers,' and let me add *some to be drama ministers . . .* 'so that the body of Christ may be built up'" (NIV).

The pastor's words that night reminded me that ministry is a two-way street, and Sandy is an example of the ministry that can and should take place among the participants. Of course, there is the more obvious ministry that transpires from the stage or platform to an audience. The ministry aspect there is most often communicated through the words and emotions—the content of the play or sketch. There can be a building-up experience for those who watch and receive.

Example No. 2: Outreach

In each performance during our dinner theatre season of five evenings, one-fourth to one-third of the audience are visitors, brought by members of the First Church family. Our advertising reads, "Dinner Drama Is a Tradition at First Church," and so it is. Part of that tradition consists of an excellent performance, a grand stage set, delicious food, and one thing more—an opportunity to be the Body of Christ to folks who may have never been with caring believers before.

For the 13 years we have performed dinner theatre, we have seen a half-dozen or so people make commitments to Christ and become part of the church. That's not a lot, but it is a better average than some of the other things we do in the name of evangelism. In one season alone, 24 individuals noted on their comment cards that they wanted to know more about life in Christ. Even after a play like *The Diary of Anne Frank,* our pastor and other ministers in town were told by parishioners that they had gone home from our performance convicted by their own intolerance and/or spiritual isolation and sought help.

One Thing More

To help the church understand the goals and sometimes successes of drama ministry, and as a testimony to us the participants, our pastor has, on occasion, had us stand as witnesses at the baptism of new Christians who had been introduced to the church by our efforts. We have been invited to do the same when any have joined the church. For us, this is a much-appreciated recognition of our ministry before the whole body. It helps validate drama to the congregation.

Validating Ministry to the Participants

In the get-acquainted meeting it will be important to emphasize the ministry concept to all who attend. You may want to use the following sketch script as a feature for the meeting. Don't bother having it memorized, just have fun with it.

The "I" in Ministry

CHAIRMAN *(stuffily):* Good evening [morning or afternoon], ladies and gentlemen. It's a pleasure to have you here. It is my privilege to inform you of the ministry opportunities of our soon to be organized drama ministry organization. But first, that reminds me . . .

WOMAN 1 *(from the audience):* OK, let's get to the point.

CHAIRMAN: Thank you, madam, I'm getting there. But first . . .

MAN 1 *(impatiently from the audience):* The lady's right, what's the point?

CHAIRMAN: The point, sir, is the fact that I am the chairman of this dramatic presentation. We have rehearsed it for three weeks *(threateningly)*, and I say you are going to enjoy it.

WOMAN 1 *(stands and comes to the front):* The flyer that I received about this meeting said that our proposed drama organization is going to be committed to quality, participation, and ministry . . .

MAN 2 *(stands and joins the woman):* She's right, and we haven't seen any quality, participation, or ministry.

WOMAN 1 *(patronizingly to* CHAIRMAN*):* Why don't you sit down and let Mr. _____, some of our friends, and me tell you what we'd like this drama group to be.

CHAIRMAN *(sitting in the audience):* Very well, madam, but don't blame me if . . .

WOMAN 1 *(interrupting):* We won't.

MAN 1: Now, if [WOMAN 2] and [MAN 2] will join us, we will present "The 'I' in Ministry."

[MUSICAL FANFARE]

WOMAN 2 *(gushing):* It's such a thrill to be part of this troupe of thespians. I've always wanted to play Juliet.

MAN 1: I beg your pardon?

WOMAN 1 *(matter-of-factly):* She says she wants to play Juliet.

MAN 2: Well, I'm not interested in being her Romeo—but Hamlet! Now that's a different story!

MAN 1: Juliet? Hamlet? Whoa. What do you folks think we're doing here?

WOMAN 2 *(lofty)*: I was the star of our third grade production of "Little Bo-Peep Meets Humpty Dumpty."

WOMAN 1: Who played Bo-Peep?

MAN 1: Haven't any of you heard of the word *ministry?*

MAN 2: Sure, that's what we pay our pastor to do.

WOMAN 2: Of course, everyone knows that. Why, when my little Fifi was sick . . .

WOMAN 1: What I believe [*name of* MAN 1] is getting at, is the fact that the drama group we are establishing [have established] has ministry as its reason for existence.

WOMAN 2: "Ministry!" Well, I never!

WOMAN 1: Yes, you will!

MAN 2: "Ministry!" Well, I'll be!

WOMAN 1: Sure, you'll be—in ministry!

MAN 1: "Ministry!" That's the word for what we aim to do through our drama organization. We will always refer to it as "our drama ministry."

WOMAN 1 *(to audience):* To help all of us keep the reason for our existence before us, we want to close with a graphic reminder of what it's all about.

(During the following each of the four actors hands a large poster of each letter to a member of the audience and brings him or her forward to hold the poster letter in order.)

MAN 1: Now we are going to involve eight of you in our ministry reminder.

(The four actors go into the audience and bring forward eight people. If there are not eight in the audience, bring four to the front of the room, and let each hold two letter posters. When the word "ministry" is displayed, begin the recitation.)

WOMAN 1: The "M" of ministry is a reminder that it's a *mandate* from God. Jesus said, "You will be my witnesses" (Acts 1:8, NIV). That's what we are going to do, because He told us to do it.

MAN 1: The "I" of ministry stands for me—that is *I.* Sometimes I don't know when to use which pronoun, but I'm sure I have to be involved in ministry.

WOMAN 2: There are things that ministry isn't. That's why the "N" stands for *not.* It's not for showing off; nor for self-satisfaction. Neither is it an exclusive clique of artistes within the church body. No, it's a for-everyone opportunity.

MAN 2: The second "I" stands for *involvement.* It is not possible for us to perform ministry unless we are involved in the whole program of this church. We need to be perceived as "Doers of the Word."

WOMAN 1: "S" stands for *service,* which is the root meaning of ministry. Our concept of ministry does not depend upon special training or exclusivity—it's service!

MAN 1: The "T" of ministry represents *talents*. Ministry is a way of facilitating people to make use of their talents in a way that will bring glory to God and the betterment of others.

WOMAN 2: The "R" in ministry is for *redeem*. Because the world has taken drama, which had its origin in the church, and turned it into an unwholesome medium of communication—we believe the church needs to redeem this powerful tool for ministry.

MAN 2: Finally "Y." I suspect you can guess what it stands for—right! It stands for *you*. Are you convinced of ministry?

WOMAN 1: Are you ready to get to work?

[At this point distribute and discuss the Interest Survey found in Appendix A in the back of this book.]

Ministry Opportunities for Drama

If the premise of the foregoing sketch is true, and that the word *ministry* means service, then it is going to be important for the church to provide these service opportunities. In an intial conversation with the pastor, make it clear that your group is not interested in becoming "prima donnas" or artistes who want to be sanctuary stars. Make yourselves available to serve the church, wherever and whenever your gifts can be utilized.

To get you started, here is a list of possible ministry/service involvements.

1. **As Sermon Enhancements.** Many of us are aware that the worship service sketch is being used throughout the church. Your pastor may be interested in involving the drama group in such a ministry on a weekly or less often schedule. Lillenas provides resources for this ministry feature in our Worship Drama Library series.

2. **For Christian Education.** Sunday School and Vacation Bible School teachers should learn to depend upon your organization for dramatic features in class, or for training children and teens to perform their own sketches and plays. For assistace in working with teens, see Tim Miller's Lillenas book, *Teens in Drama Ministry.* It is one title in the Drama Topics Series. Other organizations, like women's and men's ministries, will be likely users of drama for their purposes. Men from my group were used at our church's men's retreat to perform the contemporary disciple monologues in Jerry Cohagan's collection, *The Carpenter's Tools.*

3. **Outreach Possibilities.** The use of drama as a tool for outreach has become a viable ministry for churches everywhere, with dinner theatre leading the way. The possibility of staging an evening of dinner theatre may be a reasonable goal toward which you can be working. As I tell in my book, *Dinner Theatre: Entertaining Outreach,* this special ministry has become a major source for reaching the community by the church in which I direct a drama ministry.

Other outreach uses of drama include: Park performances in the summer; services at rescue missions, jails, and other institutions. Some church theatre groups have regularly scheduled dates at missions and jails. It becomes an important part of their sense of ministry.

3.

TAKE SERIOUSLY THE NECESSITY OF PREPARING A PURPOSE STATEMENT

If you are convinced that there is value in providing a regularly scheduled meeting for your drama ministry group—a meeting for training, fellowship, study, and inspiration—your next step is to compose a purpose or mission statement. This process is not an academic exercise, but its resulting document will clearly delineate why you exist as a ministry organization. The church will judge your ongoing ministry goals from this statement, and it should become a guideline for your choices and activities.

Exact wording of such a statement will depend upon your week-by-week expectations. The following are general considerations that might be localized and included in your purpose/mission/ministry statement.

The Purpose Statement

An attempt to summarize all that you plan to do in a paragraph is futile. Such a statement is not a detailed enumeration of all your hopes, dreams, and aspirations; instead, it is a distillation of your goals for drama as a ministry within your church and beyond. The following are a few of the many such statements that have been shared with *Lillenas Drama Newsletter*.

"It is our purpose to proclaim God-inspired truth through the medium of drama; declaring, illustrating, and clarifying biblical truth."

"Realizing that drama is proclamation, the *[group name]* of *[church name]* declares that we will communicate the many facets of life in Christ, through the various dramatic mediums made available to us."

"In the spirit of the apostle Paul, who said, 'I have become all things to all men so that by all possible means I might save some' (1 Corinthians 9:22, NIV), the drama ministry group of *[church name]* has accepted Christian theatre as a ministry, so that we too might 'win some.'"

"We, the drama ministry of *[church name]*, believe that our God-directed purpose is to influence men and women, boys and girls, with the claims of Christ. This we will do through the various dramatic arts, both religious and so-called secular; in church and out."

"Because our purpose is ministry, the *[group name]* of *[church name]* will use the dramatic arts to reach in, reach out, reach up, and reach down with the truth of scripture, expressed on stage and off; through scripts and our personal lives."

"Our goal is to give glory to the Lord Jesus Christ through the use of dramatic presentations. As an extension of our church's outreach ministries, *[name of drama group]* seeks to proclaim both the word of the Lord and the truths implied therein through drama. Our theme verse: 'We proclaim him, admonishing and teaching everyone with all wisdom, so that we may present everyone perfect in Christ' (Colossians 1:28, NIV)."

Considerations for writing purpose statements

1. Make a list of everything you and your planning group would like to see happen through your organization. Such as:

    a. Provide a sense of ministry for all who participate.

    b. Give members of our group a chance to participate in a number of different experiences in the dramatic arts and related crafts.

    c. Reach out to the artistic and show them that the church has a place for them and wants to help them commit their talents to God.

    d. Provide a spiritual environment in which group members can express their defeats as well as victories, and feel confident that their fellow members are part of their cloud of witnesses.

    e. Help the pastoral staff and church board become aware of the outreach, worship, training, as well as entertainment possibilities of drama.

And so on.

2. You might also include short-, medium-, and long-range goals that include dreams of staging specific plays, acquirement of equipment, scope of ministry, and more.

3. Make an attempt to consolidate the goals list into a paragraph, the shorter the better.

4. Find a scripture that expresses your ideals for the group. Let that verse(s) serve as an inspiration for your ministry.

There are probably other concepts to be included that are unique to your situation.

Ministry Guidelines

To help establish the standards by which your group will operate, it is wise to compose a detailed outline of what is expected of individual members of the troupe, as well as of the group as a whole. The following is a synthesis of a number of such documents.

The Drama Ministry Team of Calvary Church
Accepts the Following Guidelines

1. Ministry is our reason for existence; therefore, members are expected to accept their responsibilities and opportunities in the spirit of Christ.

2. We understand that we are a church-sponsored group, and that we are accountable to the church's Education Committee [or whatever is applicable].

3. Because of this accountability factor, scripts for performance and group plans will be cleared with the proper committee or council.

4. As part of our accountability to the church, we will submit a written report monthly to the church board through the Education Committee.

5. We understand that our ministry is two-faceted:

    a. We minister to one another as participants.

    b. We minister to our audiences and congregations.

6. Because ours is a ministry organization, we feel that the individual lifestyles of our participants need to reflect the Lord we are proclaiming.

Lillenas would be pleased to receive a copy of your purpose statements and guidelines. Please mail a set to us at:

Lillenas Drama Resources
P.O. Box 419527
Kansas City, MO 64141

THE DRAMA MEETING: A COUPLE OF GENERAL THOUGHTS, INCLUDING A PASTOR'S WORDS ON ACCOUNTABILITY

Before discussing the specific features of your drama group meetings, here are a few general reflections.

1. One hour is not enough time to do all that you will want to do in the meeting. Ninety minutes would be ideal. My group meets from 7:00 to 8:15. I wish we had 15 more minutes.

2. Start on time. Don't wait for a "full house." Because your interests are performance-oriented, the group—tech people and actors—must understand the importance of punctuality. Besides, if they know you will wait, they will always be tardy.

3. Our time allotments are: Devotions, 15 minutes; and the rest of the activities, 60 minutes.

4. I prepare a handout for each meeting. It includes the evening agenda, announcements, news, and future schedule. This keeps me organized. See a sample in the back of this book.

5. We have had success in scheduling "enrichment" trips to attend community theatre performances as a group. One evening about a dozen of us attended the performance of a great American classic play—known and loved by all. As a kind gesture to a visiting drama group, we were given prime front row center seats. Usually we would covet those seats, but as it turned out, they became a liability. Some of the actors' performances were quite bad; it was all we could do to keep from showing our amusement—and the play didn't have a comedic line in it. Later, over pie and coffee, we had a helpful discussion on what the problems were. ("But for the grace of God . . ." we all agreed.) A few months later we were back to see *Inherit the Wind*, performed by the same organization. What a difference! For the most part, the acting was very good and the set was outstanding. Even actors who had been in the previous show looked better in this one. At our pie and coffee rehash afterward, we discussed the differences and what we would have done differently. Next month we attend a free one-man performance of *The Gospel of Luke*, sponsored by InterVarsity at a community college. These "field trips" have been profitable, as well as lots of fun.

6. On occasion, mail or distribute on Sunday a reminder of the upcoming meeting and its feature. There's a copy of one I've used with the First Drama Ensemble in Appendix B. Organization, planning, and promotion cannot be over-

emphasized. The drama meeting will succeed if your group feels you are organized and taking it seriously.

7. Don't be troubled by some participants who will drop out for a period of time. These folks often want to go back to other activities that may be meeting at the same time. I face it with choir, youth groups, and Bible studies that are in operation during our Wednesday evening meeting.

8. From the first meeting, underscore the importance of accountability to oneself, the group, the church, and God. The following is an extracted portion of an address by Rev. Jesse Middendorf, my pastor, who delivered these words as a keynote address to the 500 conferees of a Lillenas Drama Conference in Kansas City. Share these words with the members of your church drama organization.

Accountability

A drama ministry must be accountable to its mission. As is the case in any evaluation of the mission of the church or any of its component parts, it must be recognized that the mission is, by its nature, varied.

1. There is a responsibility to tell the story.
2. Drama may have a mission to persuade.
3. Its mission may at times be to warn.
4. Drama may well be intended to entertain.
5. And, drama may intend to offer a wholesome outlet for the use of gifts and abilities.

There is a special sense in which the Church and its drama ministry must be accountable to the culture around it. In no other ministry is there more meaningful opportunity to speak in terms and symbols the culture understands. It is in the interaction between the Church and the culture where drama ministries may speak appealingly or prophetically in ways the secular mind can hear, while yet maintaining a deep and authentic commitment to the mission and the message of the Church.

Such a commitment necessarily presupposes the need for careful personal accountability to dependable others for one's lifestyle and self-expression. We need to remember the admonition given young Timothy by the apostle Paul: "Watch your life and doctrine closely" (1 Timothy 4:16, NIV).

Given the level of emotional investment necessary to stage drama well, it is crucial that objective accountability structures be in place.

In order to establish such accountability, there must be *intentional* structures in place. It is necessary to establish a system of personal accountability between the members of the drama ministry team. This will require willingness on the part of everyone to be

1. Vulnerable to the system
2. Open to its care
3. Sensitive to the integrity of the entire ministry

It is also necessary to establish a system of accountability between the ministry and the larger community of faith. Be willing to bring the ministry under the appropriate authority structures of the sponsoring church, offering the church better use of drama ministries across the entire spectrum of its ministries. Rather than an isolated ministry acting as a mere appendage, drama ministries should become a larger part of the whole:

1. Contributing to the expanding mission of the church
2. Assisting it to expand its borders

3. Offering new avenues of involvement to a host of people whose gifts and abilities find joyous fulfillment in this phase of the Kingdom.

Accountability must go beyond these issues. What about accountability to the authors and publishers of drama resources? The ease with which copies of published works can be made has created a credibility crisis in the Church of Jesus Christ.

Dear friends, limited resources and a desire to minister are not sufficient justification to pirate copyrighted material in any form for any purpose. That is a violation of Christian integrity. You cannot credibly represent a holy God with stolen material.

Ladies and gentlemen, I am calling for integrity. I challenge you to remember that drama ministry in the church demands the same level of integrity and holiness that should characterize every other dimension of God's kingdom. Integrity is that seamless tapestry that must run throughout all that the Church is and does; in all its various ministries and expressions—including drama.

5.

THE DRAMA MEETING: PROVIDING INSPIRATION

In planning for the inspirational/worship times in your drama ministry team meetings, keep in mind the necessity of prayerfully planning those minutes as carefully as the performance-related activities.

Because our First Drama Ensemble meets on Wednesday evenings while some of the church is in Bible studies or a prayer and praise service, it seemed important to provide a meaningful worship/devotional time in our weekly meetings. In all honesty, there are times when these devotional quarter-hours have overshadowed the other 60 minutes.

Through trial and error we have arrived at a handful of conclusions relating to the devotional time.

1. Since there is a common bond already established between many in the group, it will be possible for a spiritual rapport to be established very quickly. Devotional activities like scripture reading and discussion, prayer requests and intercession, burden sharing and bearing will assume greater importance because of the group's united commitment to the ministry of drama.

2. For most groups, the first activity of the evening is devotions. That opening feature needs to begin promptly.

3. To ensure a free exchange of personal reactions and prayer needs, we enter into a covenant with one another; personal matters shared are considered confidential and are not discussed outside of the group.

As was implied earlier, the law of homogeneous groupings is true for drama ministry groups. For us, prayer requests and subsequent sessions of prayer have contributed to a bonding within the group that cannot be programmed. It's probably the result of long rehearsal sessions and sink-or-swim performances.

Some Hints for Planning Devotions

1. Prepare a calendar of devotional presenters. Because of the value of continuity, we schedule volunteers for three-week stints.

2. With our group, we have learned that the extemporaneous sharing of personal spiritual discoveries is always meaningful. Other formats have included:

a. An avid reader may share something that he or she is currently reading, including a devotional book report.

b. A meaningful quarter-hour was recently spent with the reading of a series of letters written by a missionary to her family at home.

c. Scripted material can be a successful way to present spiritual truth. It may be original, or a meaningful play cutting.

d. Related to "c" above, you might consider a completely scripted worship experience. Mine often include scripture arrangements, short sketches, and slots for prayer and sharing. (See 5 below.)

3. My writing colleague, Jeff Wyatt [we authored *The Word in Worship* together], is preparing a book of devotionals for use by drama ministry groups. All of the devotional outlines include scripture readings, with one series based on acting and/or theatre themes.

4. During Lent and Advent, I have made use of appropriate scenes from videotaped movies, including: *Ben Hur, Jesus of Nazareth, King of Kings, Godspell, The Greatest Story Ever Told, Cotton Patch Gospel*, etc. Those listed above and others have excellent Nativity and/or Holy Week scenes. Comparing the film script with the Bible narrative, costuming, props, and characterization can make for some interesting discussion, as well as scripture insight.

5. Scripted worship has the benefit of involvement by everyone in the group. The following is a scripted worship service prepared for a Lillenas Drama Conference. It may be too long to fit into our 15-minute devotional slot, but it gives an idea of what can be done. The original had hymns and choruses interspersed. They have been eliminated in this sample.

A Scripted Worship Service

Theme: Ministry

Introductory Remarks . . . . Leader
    More than a statement in the church directory, is the truth that ours is a drama ministry, and *ministry* is the operative word. This evening we are reexamining the concept of ministry in the context of the apostle Paul and Timothy.

Drama Interlude 1 . . . . Paul Miller and Jeff McElroy

PAUL: And you, young man, what's your name?

TIM: Timothy, sir.

PAUL: Are you a believer?

TIM: A believer, sir?

PAUL: Yes, a believer in Jesus Christ. Does His Spirit live in you?

TIM: Oh, yes, sir. I became a Christian while you were preaching in Lystra. Since then, I have been taught the things of God by my mother and grandmother.

PAUL: They wouldn't be Lois and Eunice, now, would they?

TIM: Why, yes, that's who they are!

PAUL: Then you must be Timothy who made such an impression on me in other days.

TIM: I don't know about the impression I made, but you are the Paul who roomed and boarded at our house (*shyly*), and who I used to pretend was my father.

PAUL: Timothy, I have heard such fine things about your commitment and influence. I can see that the Lord has laid His hand on you.

TIM: The Lord has been better to me than I deserve.

PAUL: Tell me, would you be willing to join me in ministry?

TIM: You mean leave Lystra and travel with you?

PAUL: That's right. You see, John Mark has left us, so Silas and I need help. I think you're the one to provide it. What do you say?

TIM *(hesitantly):* Before I say yes, Paul, would you tell me something?

PAUL: Of course, anything.

TIM: Why did John Mark decide to leave the ministry?

PAUL *(with a note of sadness):* Well, son, I believe he is no longer with us because of a disagreement in which I became impatient and boorish. But, I've learned a lesson or two from that experience. As my dear old friend Barnabas said, "one of the fruit of living in Christ is patience."

TIM: Well, then, what else can I say but *yes!* I'll join you and Silas in ministry. But one thing more . . .

PAUL: What's that?

TIM: In school we were taught that when in a job interview, ask the senior pastor what his concept of ministry is. So, Paul, what is ministry to you?

PAUL *(warmly):* Oh my, I've wrestled with that question for many years. I recall, as if it happened yesterday, the event that started my process of ministry. It started with the murder of a young man named Stephen, whose spirit actually ministered to me while he was being stoned in Jerusalem, and culminated in my blindness and eventual new birth in Damascus. It was while in Damascus that I was ministered to by a brother named Ananias. From Stephen and Ananias and a host of other believers I learned the possibility of ministry. It may wear different cloaks, but its common denominator is to love people and look at them through the eyes of Christ Jesus. That's what I expect from you, Timothy.

Scripture Reading . . . . 2 Timothy 4:1-5

LEADER: In the presence of God and of Christ Jesus, . . . I give you this:

GROUP: Preach the Word,

WOMEN: Be prepared in season and out of season;

MEN: Correct,

WOMEN: Rebuke and encourage—

GROUP: With great patience and careful instruction.

LEADER: Keep your head in all situations,

MEN: Endure hardships,

WOMEN: Do the work of an evangelist,

GROUP: Discharge all the duties of your ministry.

Drama Interlude 2 . . . . Paul Miller and Jeff McElroy

LEADER: The scene is a subterranean prison cell in Rome. The apostle Paul is chained to an iron ring in the wall. He sits at a writing desk. Out of sight in an anteroom, Paul hears the grate of an iron door opening and then a familiar voice speaks.

LUKE: I'm the prisoner's physician. Please let me go in to see my patient.

PAUL: Is that you, Luke?

LUKE: It's me, Paul. You are *still* writing.

PAUL: Yes, I have a lot to say to my son Timothy.

LUKE: You've been at this one for a long while, Paul.

PAUL: I know, and I'm savoring every minute of it. As I write, I keep remembering the day Timothy asked me about my concept of ministry. I think he knows, don't you, Doc?

LUKE: So, old man, are you ready for your last journey?

PAUL: If you mean on foot or by a creaking ocean tub, the answer is "No!" *(Warmly)* But if you mean my final journey that takes me to the One whose prisoner I am, the answer is a resounding "Yes!"

LUKE: When will you see Timothy again, Paul?

PAUL: On this side, I'm not sure. Perhaps I need to tell him to come quickly. Winter is about on us, and I don't think I can endure this leaking cistern without my coat and some books.

LUKE: What can I do, Paul?

PAUL *(distracted):* Hmm?

LUKE: I'd like to make your days a little more comfortable, if I can.

PAUL: Thank you, Luke. You take good care of my body. I have the Father for my soul. Now I need Timothy for my heart's sake.

Scripture Reading . . . . 2 Timothy 4:6-8

LEADER: The apostle Paul continues: I am already being poured out like a drink offering, and the time has come for my departure.

MEN: I have fought the good fight,

LEADER: I have finished the race,

WOMEN: I have kept the faith.

GROUP: Now there is in store for me a crown of righteousness,

LEADER: Which the Lord, the righteous Judge, will award me on that day—

GROUP: Not only to me, but also to all who have longed for his appearing.

Scripture Interpretation . . . . Group
    Be ready to discuss these words of Paul in the light of drama ministry.

Prayer Requests and Petitions . . . . Leader and Group

Response . . . . Chorus

> *I need Thee; O I need Thee!*
> *Ev'ry hour I need Thee!*
> *O bless me now, my Savior;*
> *I come to Thee!*

A Unison Affirmation . . . . Psalm 19:14
    May the words of my mouth and the meditation of my heart be pleasing in your sight, O Lord, my Rock and my Redeemer.

[Note: If you reproduce the above, be sure the following credit line is included.]

In Conclusion

In the heat of creative planning, don't allow your minutes of devotions to become performances. There must be time for sharing and caring. Naturally, some times will lend themselves more to that than other times. Always request prayer concerns; let the group share family needs, and encourage them to report answers to prayer and other blessings. If your volunteer devotions leader would prefer, let someone else handle the prayer requests and prayer time.

Above all, allow this period of time to be meaningful. Give opportunity for silence as well as speaking, contributing as well as proclaiming, seeking as well as finding.

6.

THE DRAMA MEETING: ACTOR TRAINING

While we need to make every effort to encourage future directors, tech people, and writers to be part of the church drama group, it is realistic to acknowledge that most people in your groups want to "trod the boards"—to act. The weekly meeting is an ideal setting for so-called acting classes.

"Wait right there. I'm not capable of teaching acting lessons; I wouldn't know what to do."

Hear me out before you react. Let's take this topic of actor training a step at a time.

Step 1: Recognize That Training
Was a Reason for an Organization

From the first you acknowledged the need to sharpen your actors' abilities. That was a major concern in setting up regular meetings.

Training does not always happen through a so-called expert lecturing from one's personal experience. Training is often the result of observation, participation, and making discoveries together.

It may be possible for you to find an instructor or teacher from a high school or community college in your area. This person may be happy to share from his or her experience for the cost of a dinner. This has been my technique in getting two different acting instructors to come to our Wednesday evening meeting. Regardless of your needs, it is always wise to get acquainted with the resources available to you from neighboring educational institutions. Last fall I discovered that the costume and prop departments of the University of Missouri at Kansas City were open to me. Their rental rates are much lower than the commercial houses, and their selections are superior.

Step 2: If You Must
Be Your Own Instructor

No need to be overly concerned if no acting instruction is available—just decide to convene the acting classes yourself. Naturally, you will not pass yourself off as a latter-day Stanislavski (a great Russian actor and coach), but you will encourage the group to join you in learning together.

What follows is an outline of some acting pointers and games that I use. You are welcome to share them with the group, including making handouts. For in-depth material I heartily recommend Robert Rucker's Lillenas text *Producing and Directing Drama in the Church.*

I. An Introduction

    A. Traditionally, a discussion of the actor's craft is divided into two categories: movement and voice.

B. The physical conduct of an actor onstage begins with an understanding of stage directions (see diagram).

C. These directions are always given from the viewpoint of the actor as he faces the audience: stage right, stage left, upstage, and downstage.

The Larger Stage

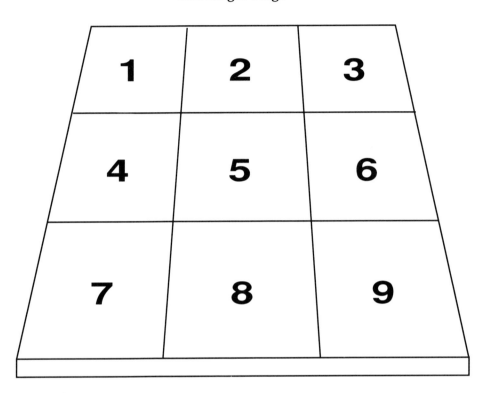

D. The nine onstage areas of the larger stage are:
1. Upstage right
2. Upstage center
3. Upstage left
4. Center stage right
5. Center stage
6. Center stage left
7. Downstage right
8. Downstage center
9. Downstage left

The Smaller Stage

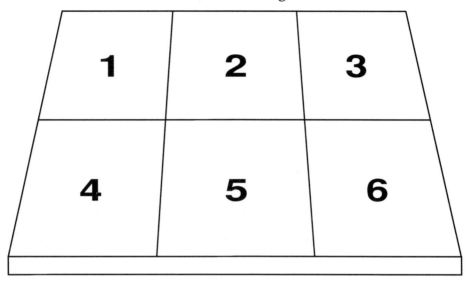

E. Smaller acting areas use these six designations:
1. Upstage right
2. Upstage center
3. Upstage left
4. Downstage right
5. Downstage center
6. Downstage left

II. Acting Is Movement
  A. What Is Movement?
    1. Movement is the actual transit of an actor from one point onstage to another.
    2. Ninety-five percent of all stage movement comes from the dramatic action in the script.
    3. Experienced actors can usually move spontaneously, but most of us in church drama will want to plot stage movement (called blocking).
  B. Movement Comes from Dramatic Action
    1. The most convincing moves in a play come from the drama itself.
    2. Nervous pacing, shifting from foot to foot, or movement that is derived from the actor not wanting to stand still delivering lines is distracting movement. Of course, if such erratic action helps characterize a role or mood, then that movement actually does spring from the dramatic action.
  C. The Basic Movements
    1. Walking: One of the most basic moves for the actor.
      a. Provides excellent opportunity to portray character.
      b. Stage walking needs to be natural, easy, and graceful (unless the actor is developing a character walk).
      c. Men and women should point toes forward, and put one foot, more or less, in front of the other. Old age can be approximated by turning the toes out and spreading the feet farther apart. Extreme old age is indicated by a shuffle.

2. Standing: Posture is extremely important. The actor's body is one of the primary means of communication.

   a. Rule for standing—head held high, shoulders back, stomach in, hips thrust forward, body weight on the balls of the feet.

   b. As an exercise, the old book-on-the-head walk works.

3. Turning: Ordinarily the actor executes a turn toward the audience, unless this appears awkward.

4. Kneeling: This move needs to be performed gracefully.

   a. Keep the torso and head upright.

   b. Always kneel on the downstage knee.

   c. Kneeling on both knees indicates extreme contrition or sorrow.

5. Sitting and Rising: These can be character-indicating moves.

   a. Tired or elderly will sit and rise in ways that indicate how they feel.

   b. Nerves dictate how the actor sits—edge of couch, etc.

6. Entrances: This action will set a mood and establish the impact of the rest of the scene.

   a. Important—The actor who enters is coming from somewhere. That needs to be kept in mind.

   b. Actor enters the scene in character. He is coming in to do something. He doesn't saunter, unless it's in character.

7. Exits: An exit can be as dramatic and telling as an entrance.

   a. The actor's exit will reflect what has just transpired in the scene—anger, hurt, loneliness, etc.

   b. Related business will underscore mood and character—reaching for the doorknob, pushing aside a person, fumbling for a key.

8. Some movement exercises for the group

   a. As you present each of the seven moves discussed above, take time to set up exercises illustrating each, that the group may participate in.

   b. Assign a Bible story, fairy tale, or nursery rhyme character to each participant. Invite each to interpret his or her character by movement alone.

III. Acting Is Speaking
   A. Spoken Dialogue Is the Heart of Storytelling
      1. Consequently, the actor must speak to be understood
      2. Projection is the ability to be heard. It gives life to a character. Projection includes:

         a. Articulation—making use of tongue, teeth, and lips.

         b. Pronunciation—a definite part of being understood. The dictionary is an ideal tool.

         c. Relaxation—tenseness makes speaking difficult to understand.

         d. Volume—not incorporated in dramatic speech as much as the inexperienced may think. Increased level of sound more often produced by articulation. Loudness cannot obliterate clarity.

         e. Confidence—security in lines will make the actor confident, which in turn projects character.

         f. Pitch—It is said that good actors do most of their speaking within a very small range pitch—maybe a three-note range. Raising pitch is for dramatic moments in a play.

         g. Head movement—When speaking, an actor generally holds his head still, but not rigid. An absolute necessity to being heard.

h. Energy—Speaking with the energy of one's whole body is the way an actor is heard and truly communicates. He or she breathes deeply, and puts every fiber of himself or herself into the character. This is projection.

      3. Some Speaking Exercises for the Group

      a. Vowels and consonants: Repeat these jingles often enough until they are no longer tongue twisters.

> The mate can make a plate of pastry cakes.
> Feed the breed with meat and wheat.
> He didn't care two hoots for the blue book.
> Coal makes smoke, but coke is smokeless.

      b. Inflection: Encourage actors to go through their scripts to discover lines that carry a number of interpretations, as these do:

> "IS this your Bible?" (Are you sure?)
> "Is THIS your Bible?" (. . . or is it THAT one?)
> "Is this YOUR Bible?" (. . . or does it belong to someone else?)
> "Is this your BIBLE?" (It looks more like a dictionary.)

IV. Acting Is Feeling

    A. Feeling: Next to being understood, the most important thing of all is the feeling behind the speech.

      1. When the script is memorized and projection is mastered, one's attention can be concentrated on the stimulation of feeling and emotion in yourself as an actor, which in turn will be communicated to the audience.

      a. Feeling dictates movement and speech.

      b. If he allows himself to feel the character, he will begin to move and speak like that character.

      c. How does an actor get that feeling?

        (1) Concentration.

        (2) Motivation and reason behind character's behavior to be thought through.

        (3) Empathy with the character.

    B. An Exercise in Character Development: Read Luke 15:11-31 and answer the following character questions about the father. The answers are not in the New Testament account; they need to come from your imagination and heart.

      1. What was the father's line of business?

      2. What did he look like? Compare him to a person whom you feel has the same physical characteristics.

      3. What was the father's initial reaction when his younger son asked for his share of the inheritance?

      4. What went through his mind relative to his older son?

      5. What did the father say to his younger son when he left for the "distant country"?

      6. When a friend reported to the father that he had seen the boy feeding pigs, what was the father's reponse?

      7. When the older son complained that his father should forget the younger boy, what was the father's answer?

      8. How did the father respond when he saw his younger son walking up the front path to the house?

    C. Prepare similar questions for the younger son, the older son, and maybe the pig farmer.

V. Acting Is Characterization: The Process of Building Characterization
  A. Intuitive Response and Study
    1. In the first reading of the play an actor will do well to make notes on his or her initial reaction to the role.
    2. Then study and research the character in detail.
    3. If the role in question is historical, then a trip to the public library is in order.
      a. Need to know customs of the period.
      b. If the script is a historical biblical play, then start with the Bible itself, then turn to Bible reference books.
  B. Textual Clues
    1. The script itself will provide insights for developing a character.
      a. Comb the script to discover what is said about the character by others in the play.
      b. Then, what does the character say about himself or herself?
      c. Even costume descriptions and some stage description will shed more light.
    2. An experienced actor notes exactly what happens to his or her character during the play and how the person changes or develops scene by scene.
  C. Use of Imagination: When historical data has been exhausted, the actor will be forced to plug into his or her imagination. He needs to ask himself or herself at least three questions.
    1. How does this character spend his days, and in what environment?
    2. How does this character see himself? How does this affect his actions?
    3. What line in the dialogue might be considered a key to understanding this character?
  D. Stage Presence: It is important to consider what the actor's character is thinking at all times, including those times when he or she silently communicates a character. This can be done through:
    1. Posture. How the individual stands or sits.
    2. Facial expression. Reactions to other characters will be reflected on the face.
    3. Gestures. A turn of the head or hand reveals a great deal about one's response to another character. Of course this can in no way be distracting.
    4. Observation. A rich source for characterization is one's own family, neighbors, and fellow workers.

Acting Exercises and Games

All work and no play will make even a drama meeting dull. Warm-up and acting exercises will add great fun for the group and will be fine learning activities. They teach creativity and improvisation, and provide opportunity for interaction. The following "games" require no preparation.

The Great Escape

Each participant has 60 seconds to escape from an imaginary place in which he or she is trapped (a pit, a closet, a cave, a car trunk, a cage, etc). The entire body should be used in a convincing manner in the attempt. Start the improvisation with one person alone. After 60 seconds, add a person to assist. Keep adding participants until a group of four or five succeeds in escaping. Discuss with participants their feelings and their choice of escape methods.

Light and Heavy Loads

Put the whole group in a circle. The leader presents an imaginary light-weight object to the first person in line, who passes it on to the next person. Leader calls out that the original article has become something heavier or lighter, bulky or whatever. The passer then assumes posture of passing new object. He or she will also reflect the weight factor in the way it is carried. Objects might be:

An egg,
    a football,
        a heavy suitcase,
            a dishpan filled to the brim with water,
                a newborn infant, etc.

Getting-a-Word-In

In this activity, participants are grouped into two-person teams and carry on simultaneous arguments on two sides of the same topic. Set up a situation that allows the two persons to be genuinely involved in a consistent line of reasoning as they argue. Both members of the team speak at the same time. This exercise develops concentration and highlights the difference between hearing and listening. Neither person can really listen to his or her partner, or the train of thought will be lost.

Tag Team

This exercise is great fun. Organize the group into teams of four people. Teams are paired (that is, two teams together). One of the teams in each group starts a mimed activity (for instance, two people playing one-on-one basketball). These two improvise the scene until one person on the other team calls out, "Freeze!" and comes out and tags one of the performing actors, who then sits down. The new person takes the exact pose of the person who left, then the scene is activated, but the new actor alters it completely. (For instance, the two people switch from playing basketball to digging a grave and end up lowering in a coffin.) Someone from the other team now calls out, "Freeze!" and tags out someone else. (Now the two people may be carrying bags of money from a bank heist.) The game must go very quickly, and most situations should not last more than 30 seconds. The real challenge is for the actor left in each situation, who must quickly adapt to the new scenario without changing character. This is a highly recommended exercise.

Visit your public library and look at other books of acting exercises and games.

7.

THE DRAMA MEETING: SCRIPT READING AND WRITING

There is only one way to find material for your group, and that is to read scripts. The serious director is always on the lookout for additions to his or her library of Lillenas Drama Resources. When you are on the drama mailing list you will automatically receive notice of new script publications through *Lillenas Drama Newsletter,* as well as receive a copy of the annual Drama and Program Resources catalog.

An enjoyable activity for the church drama group can be an evening of script reading. The reading process is good on a couple of levels.

1. It is a nonthreatening time when everybody reads together—actor, tech person, visitor, and anyone else. No one is judged for his or her ability. The script is the center of attention.

2. The director is allowed to hear how a spoken script sounds. Too often we have to select a script that has been heard only through the ear of the mind. Turning the group loose on a series of sketches or a longer play also provides an opportunity for you to hear how well someone reads who has been hiding in a costume closet, too shy to come out for an audition. Of course you will make a mental note of that kind of newfound talent.

Script Selection

Any kind of script may be used for a reading night. The number of characters and scenes are immaterial. Usually we do not take time to edit out any "no-no's" that might show up; the actors perform this function as they read. (Of course, if you stay with Lillenas scripts, you will have nothing to bleep out.)

This may be the place to comment on how to select script for performance (not for reading nights—where a cast of thousands will work as well as a monologue—maybe better).

Consider these issues when selecting a script for performance:

1. Do I have the physical resources to stage this work: number of performers and correct genders; a stage that will facilitate the production; lighting equipment to do it justice?

2. Do I have the financial resources for performance fees (royalty payment); script purchase; costume construction or rental? (Remember, period works are expensive to costume.)

3. Will this script hold up with my audience: Will they understand it; is it theologically appropriate for my group?

For a let's-see-what-this-is-all-about reading, though, you don't have to be concerned with these cautions.

How to Group-Read Script

On script reading evenings, our group sits around the usual square of tables. Each person has a copy of the script(s) to be read. Caution: You cannot reproduce any copyrighted script. However, if you write or call for permission, some publishers will allow you to photocopy a script for reading purposes. Usually the publisher requests that copyright information be included on each copy; and that you promise to destroy the copies after the reading. Of course, if you decide to stage the work, it is imperative that you purchase a copy for each actor and the directing staff members.

The reading procedure is simple—we read around the circle without designating characters. I, or someone else, reads stage directions. It's surprising how well participants will get into the spirit of the play, even reading a different character at each turn. As director, I usually spend time discussing some of the following with the group after the reading.

1. Are the individual characters believable?
2. Is the play appropriate for our kind of audiences?
3. Would you enjoy participating in a production of this work?
4. If we were to select this play for production, which role(s) would you audition for?
5. If we were to stage this work, are there any alterations that we would need to make to the script?
6. Is the plot line easy to follow?
7. How do the characters and plot situations hold up to today's social concerns?
8. Is this play primarily entertainment, or is there an underlying message in the work?
9. Is the play consistent with a Christian point of view?
10. Where is the play's climax?

Script Writing

Surprisingly, an activity that met with favorable response by my drama group were three sessions on script writing. These were not seminars on sketch writing, but they provided a taste of creative writng, which in turn has spurred a person or two to go on and try their hand at serious writing.

What follows is a brief outline for a group exercise in sketch writing.

1. Your Preparation

   a. Secure a selection of preaching texts from your pastor.

   b. Or select your own scripture texts or themes.

   c. Prepare a handout for the group that contains these scriptures or themes. Also include an outline of the writing process they will experience.

2. First Session

   a. Discuss the value of learning what goes into writing a script, even if one has no plans to become a playwright.

      (1) Helps the actor better appreciate the script he or she is investing time in.

      (2) Provides technician with the same.

      (3) Gives everyone some tools for ministry, in that they may be able to create their own skits and sketches.

(4) While Lillenas and others provide a broad variety of scripts, it isn't always possible to find a suitable presentation, so why not try your hand at writing your own script?

b. What makes a sketch a sketch as opposed to a play?

(1) Usually a limited number of characters.

(2) Presents one central idea, though there may be lesser ideas expressed or inferred.

(3) There is an introduction, in which characters are met; the main body, when a problem is introduced and the characters must struggle with solving it; the conclusion, which provides the solution to the problem. There can be variations on this basic scheme.

(4) The opening or introduction ought to grab the audience's attention immediately.

(5) The closing needs to provide a strong curtain line to wrap up the sketch.

(6) In a worship sketch, it is often advisable not to provide a neat solution to the problem created. That may become the responsibility of the one who speaks following. (The preacher will provide a preference.)

c. Distribute the sheet of scripture references and explain why these specific verses were selected. If you are writing sketches to accompany sermons, it may be wise to invite your pastor to the meeting to explain the whys and hows of his sermon texts.

d. The first writing project will consist of preparing a treatment of the sketch that will be created.

(1) A treatment is the telling of the sketch, written as a short story. It tells how the sketch will be treated or handled.

(2) Before writing the scenario or story of your sketch, take time to express its theme in an introductory sentence or two.

(3) If time and resources permit, read background information about the scripture from a Bible commentary.

(4) A treatment usually does not include dialogue, but describes what the characters say.

e. Give the group an hour or so in which to write treatments. If time permits, invite members of the group to read their treatments.

3. Next Session

a. Pass out copies of an actual sketch script (see Appendix D). Discuss what a script must contain, using the sample script.

(1) Title

(2) Theme

(3) Cast and prop lists

(4) Description of the setting

(5) Where the characters are and what they are doing when the play starts.

(6) Then comes the body of the play, which consists of

(a) Dialogue by characters

(b) Descriptions of movement

(c) Technical instructions regarding lights, sound, and so on.

(7) There are times when a sketch is divided into scenes. Incidentally, there should not be major scene or prop changes between scenes of a short sketch. Scene divisions more often than not represent time changes, not locations.

b. Some words about dialogue

(1) Let conversation (dialogue) carry as much of the story as possible. There are times when a narrator provides information that dialogue can't. The use of a narrator should be resisted.

(2) Keep dialogue spare. Don't write long speeches, unless it is part of the characterization. Even then, there are other ways of implying long-windness.

(3) Remember, speech can define characterization.

(a) Not everyone speaks in complete sentences all the time.

(b) Some people use poor grammar, others drop the "g" at the end of "ing" words, still others don't use contractions—like "don't." Keep from making everyone speak like an English text.

(4) Don't allow biblical characters to speak like the King James Version of the Bible.

(5) Provide the actor or interpretor with clues on how a line should be spoken. Such instruction is include within the speech, separated by parentheses.

4. Subsequent Sessions. If the schedule permits, allow for writing time during the weekly meeting; if not, encourage those who are interested to write at home and bring their work to be read in the meeting.

You will want to keep your eyes and ears open for participants who show ability in writing. Let your pastor know of such talent.

Lillenas is producing two books on writing that will be of interest. The first is on sketch script writing and production (MP-517), by Mike Gray. The second is how to write one-act or full-length play scripts (MP-760), by Paul McCusker.

8.

THE DRAMA MEETING: SOME TECH TALK

If your group meets weekly it will (or has) become evident that there needs to be activities on the meeting schedule in addition to script reading, acting classes, and devotions.

The mysterious area of backstage business—primarily the technical side of the business—needs to be investigated by the group. Hopefully there are some budding technicians present; not everyone needs to play Hamlet. Thank goodness for the folks who are willing to learn the intricacies of stage lighting, makeup—both regular and character, sound enhancement, and set design and construction. There are some excellent sets of video training tapes that relate to many of these same tech crafts. Most are rather pricey, but they are taught by experts. For information and catalogs contact:

Theatre Video Series
D.V.C., Inc.
P.O. Box 30054
Indianapolis, IN 46230
317-575-8015

Theatre Arts Video Library
174 Andrew Ave.
Leucadia, CA 92024
1-800-456-8285; FAX 619-632-6355

Lighting

Drama group meetings are a natural place to introduce tech topics. If there is a theatrical equipment outlet in your town, pay it a visit and invite the lighting specialist over to your meeting. Ask if he or she will bring some lighting instruments, a dimmer board, and a tree. It will make for an interesting meeting to have an equipment demonstration. Usually such an agency has gel swatch books, catalogs, and other literature to give away.

Do your homework, director, and make a trip to the library and pick up some of the excellent theatrical lighting books you'll find there. Also, secure a copy of Robert Rucker's Lillenas how-to book, *Producing and Directing Drama for the Church*. If no lighting technician is available to you, make notes from the Rucker book for handouts, and discover-learn with the group. One other source for technical assistance is a community college or high school.

You may contact leading lighting suppliers directly and request descriptive materials. In a cover letter, explain the purpose of your drama group and the tech subjects you are exploring. Here is a partial list of theatrical lighting companies.

Rosco [For color gels and patterns]
1135 N. Highland Ave.
Hollywood, CA 90038
1-800-767-2669

The Great American Market [For gels, patterns, effects]
826 N. Cole Ave.
Hollywood, CA 90038

Altman Stage Lighting Co., Inc.
57 Alexander St.
Yonkers, NY 10701
914-476-7987; FAX 914-963-7304

Premier Lighting & Production
11319 Vanowen St.
North Hollywood, CA 91605-6321
818-762-0884; FAX 818-762-0896

Colortran
1015 Chestnut St.
Burbank, CA 91506
818-843-1200; FAX 818-972-5599

Associated Theatrical Contractors
307 W. 80th
Kansas City, MO 64114
816-523-1655

Makeup

Again, a makeup expert may be available from a theatrical supply house in town, or from the staff of an area college or high school. If such is not available, again, discover-learn with the members of the group.

Make a trip to the public library and pick up a book or two on the subject. Or, contact one of the major theatrical makeup houses and ask for any material they can supply—preferably without charge! You might also inquire about student makeup kits that are often quite inexpensive. The leading makeup houses can be contacted through these addresses.

Ben Nye Co.
5935 Bowcroft St.
Los Angeles, CA 90016
213-893-1984; FAX 213-839-2640

Bob Kelly
151 W. 46th St.
New York, NY 10036
212-819-0030; FAX 212-869-0396

Mehron Inc.
45 E. Rte. 303
Valley Cottage, NY 10989
1-800-332-9955; FAX 914-268-0439

The whole question of theatrical makeup can be summarized in the statement, "We use it in order to look natural under stage lighting." That really doesn't tell the whole story, but its point is true.

Michael and Ginger Shew, makeup artists whom we use in the annual Lillenas drama conference say: "Why do we use makeup?

1. To set mood or character
2. To enhance visibility
3. To accommodate stage lighting"

You will find a helpful makeup chart and form in the back of this book. It may be reproduced for your group.

Costuming

As with the other technical disciplines, it is impossible to provide a how-to manual on costume design and production in this publication. Again, the Rucker book *Producing and Directing Drama for the Church* is an excellent starting point for such a discussion with your group, as are many other texts available from the library. You may want to request catalogs and other information from these sources:

Lacey Costume Wig
249 W. 34th St., Suite 707
New York, NY 10001
1-800-562-9911; FAX 212-967-4524

The Scarlet Thread
9525 Blind Pass Rd., Suite 1204
St. Petersburg Beach, FL 33706
813-367-5153

Carol's Costumes [Biblical]
Rte. 1, Box 105
Aurora, NE 68818
402-694-3309

Garments of Galilee, Inc. [Biblical]
15329 E. 13th St.
Tulsa, OK 74108
918-437-5330

Among the forms in the Appendix of this book, you will find some costuming charts that your group will want to become familiar with. It would be good to divide the group into teams of two to take measurements. Be sure to have a supply of tape measures on hand for this activity.

Oh, Yes . . .

Do not let a limited knowledge of the technical side of church theatre keep you from introducing the topic in your meetings. Undoubtedly there will be participants who have genuine interest in the various crafts: lighting, makeup, costumes, and so on. Let these folk do independent research and study, then invite them to share what they have learned with the whole group.

After scores of years, I have finally learned that an important quality of drama ministry leadership is the ability to admit to areas of "un-expertise," and have the good sense to allow others to shine.

SOME FINAL THOUGHTS

Since beginning this writing project, I have been involved in my various ongoing drama ministry responsibilities for my church and for Lillenas: leading a dozen Wednesday night meetings, putting together a cutting from the play *From Out of the Whirlwind*, directing the annual Lillenas Drama Conference.

During these experiences, I have tried to rethink what I believe about drama as a ministry. I have to occasionally ask myself, "When I'm in the thick of it, am I really as committed to the concept as I am when I'm conducting a workshop or sitting at my word processing keyboard?"

I am.

In fact, all of the above have made me even more dedicated to this form of ministry. It works.

Scene 1

(A week ago Wednesday night. It was a script reading evening. As the group gathered, DEBBIE rushed in and came directly to me.)

DEBBIE: Is my friend here yet?

P.M.M.: Your friend?

DEBBIE: Yes, my friend Kayla, who works in my office, is interested in drama, so I told her about our church and what we're doing here.

P.M.M.: And she wants to visit us?

DEBBIE: Exactly.

(At that moment, in walked Kayla, DEBBIE's friend. She has attended every meeting for eight weeks—even has brought her husband.)

Scene 2

(Two of us are sitting around the rehearsal room after a couple-of-hours workout interpreting Job, his four comforting friends, and Satan. The other person, who has asked not to be identified, had something on his mind.)

PERSON *(repeating the title of the work)*: Out of the Whirlwind—man, I'd say so!

P.M.M.: Had a work out?

PERSON: You better believe it.

P.M.M.: You enjoy our drama ministry, don't you?

PERSON: Besides our dinner theatre, I think I anticipate the Wednesday evening meeting like little else.

P.M.M.: I suppose you know I'm writing a Lillenas book on this topic?

PERSON: Of course, you've talked about it enough.

(*Director friend, expect to get little respect from your friends in this ministry.*)

P.M.M.: So, what's on your mind?

PERSON: There are so many lines in this scene we're working on that relate directly to me. The character I'm playing is almost me, at least I've heard myself say some of the things he says.

P.M.M. (*thinking of this writing project*): Ah, the mirror that is theatre.

(*We'll draw the curtain on this scene to protect confidentiality.*)

Scene 3

(*A question-and-answer session at our February drama conference. Among the 500 conferees amassed in the auditorium, a young lady with a Texas way of speaking stands to ask a question.*)

P.M.M.: Yes, miss. You have a question for one of our panel members?

TEXAN: I have one for you.

P.M.M. (*warily*): What's that?

TEXAN: I'm so tired of having to start over again at the close of every performance. Isn't there some way we can build on past performances? Seems to me that there must be some way to hold our group together.

(*And so we are back to where we started—the whole purpose of this book. Please let me hear from you. Write and describe the drama ministry you are part of. P.M.M.*)

APPENDIXES

A. Drama Ministry Group Information Sheet
B. Sample Drama Group Handout
C. Sample Audition Form
D. Sample Sketch Script
E. Makeup Chart
F. Costume Fitting Chart—Male
G. Costume Fitting Chart—Female

DRAMA MINISTRY GROUP
INFORMATION SURVEY

[Note: The numerical designations are for computer records.]

Name _____ Age ___ Birthday _____

Address _____

City, State, ZIP _____

Home phone _____

Day phone _____

(If a work number, can you receive calls? Yes___ No___)

Single___ Married___ Spouse's name _____

Children's names _____

1. I am interested in the following opportunities. Check all that apply:

   [ ]   (1.1)   Acting
   [ ]   (1.2)   Directing
   [ ]   (1.3)   Lighting
   [ ]   (1.4)   Set design
   [ ]   (1.5)   Set construction
   [ ]   (1.6)   Makeup
   [ ]   (1.7)   Prop selection
   [ ]   (1.8)   Prop management
   [ ]   (1.9)   Stage management
   [ ]   (1.10)   Music selection
   [ ]   (1.11)   Music performance
   [ ]   (1.12)   Costume selection
   [ ]   (1.13)   Costume construction
   [ ]   (1.14)   Costume care and management
   [ ]   (1.15)   Poster making
   [ ]   (1.16)   Ticket sales
   [ ]   (1.17)   Program preparation
   [ ]   (1.18)   Program ad sales
   [ ]   (1.19)   Computer record keeping
   [ ]   (1.20)   Script writing

[ ]   (1.21)   Stage crew

[ ]   (1.22)   Assisting director

Other _____

2. I am usually available for rehearsals on:

[ ]   (2.1)   Sunday afternoon

[ ]   (2.2)   Monday evening

[ ]   (2.3)   Tueday evening

[ ]   (2.4)   Wednesday evening

[ ]   (2.5)   Thursday evening

[ ]   (2.6)   Friday evening

[ ]   (2.7)   Saturday morning

[ ]   (2.8)   Saturday afternoon

[ ]   (2.9)   Saturday evening

3. I have performing experience in the following kinds of roles:

[ ]   (3.1)   Dramatic

[ ]   (3.2)   Comedic

[ ]   (3.3)   Older character

[ ]   (3.4)   Younger character

[ ]   (3.5)   Singing

[ ]   (3.6)   Dancing

4. Plays/musicals in which I have performed (role) _____

_____

_____

In signing this form I am indicating that I am willing to enter into a covenant relationship with the members of this group, and that I understand that ministry is at the heart of all we do.

_____
Signature

_____
Date

SAMPLE DRAMA GROUP HANDOUT

Wed. Nite Drama

KCF Drama Ensemble • Wednesday, January 20, 1993

LET IT SNOW, let it snow, let it snow," is how last week's sheet began. Note, the rerun. Thanks for being here. Someone in authority asked how we were able to have such consistently good attendance? My answer? "Commitment, my friend, commitment." Besides, we like what we're doing.

Tonight's Concerns

Devotions .... **Timothy Crutcher**

When Tim's tall and lanky frame made itself known, soon after arriving for seminary from SNU, it was obvious that the person who belonged to that afore-mentioned body was a committed thespian, and was entitled to all the honors accorded that commitment. Wife Rhonda is at his usually at his side. She is a tekkie at heart. And now, here's Tim!

Acting Class .... **Dr. Deborah Craig-Claar**

Because I did not read this intro last week, I am reprinting it so I can be sure you've read it. For you who are meeting Deborah for the first time, you need to know that she is a recent Ph.D. from the University of Missouri; author of What Do You Do with the Second Shepherd on the Left?, published by Lillenas; teaches theatre and public speaking at Penn Valley Community College; directs church and community theatre groups; will be teaching advanced acting classes at the Lillenas Drama Conference.

DEATH TAKES A HOLIDAY this Friday night at Kansas City KS Community College Performing Arts Center. Meet at the church at 6:30. The play starts at 8:00 pm, but we'll need to purchase tickets. Price per ticket is $5.00.

OUR NEXT SUNDAY EVE. sketch is February 14. Pastor wants a valentine/love theme. Thanks to last Sunday's team for a fine job: director Tim, actors Marilyn and Thurman, and stage manager Shirley, who learned to climb the ladder to the crows nest and operate the follow spot.

TOURING GROUP Task Force met last Sunday evening. It was agreed that we will cast and rehearse BRIDGE OF BLOOD, offer it to our church for a missionary performance, and then make available to churches in the area. Two churches with NPH contacts have already requested us. Next Wednesday night we will work on BRIDGE OF BLOOD during our 7:00 meeting.

DINNER DRAMA, 1993 was announced last week. The dates are October 22, 23, 28, 29, 30. The play, "Our Town" by Thorton Wilder. We will have a read through this spring and a viewing of a televised near-stage version, lent by Mark Marvin.

DRAMA GROUP AUDITION FORM
SNAPSHOTS AND PORTRAITS

Name _____ Child _____ Adult _____

Address _____ Teen _____ Senior ____

City, State, ZIP _____

Home phone _____ Day phone _____

(If a work number, can you receive calls? Yes___ No___)

REHEARSAL SCHEDULE
Our rehearsal schedule will probably be as follows:
Sundays   2:00 - 6:00 P.M. (Family potluck weekly)
Wednesday 6:30 - 7:30 P.M.
Saturday   9:00 -12:00 M. (Breakfast/devotions at 9:00)

First rehearsal will be Wed., August 16.
Performances will be October 22, 23, 28, 29, 30.

I have read the rehearsal schedule and, if selected, will commit myself to it.

_____
Signature

AUDITION INFORMATION
Please indicate the roles you wish to read. Note the script pages where each character appears. We will select audition scenes from these.

Cast

___ Sharon Forbes	A single	Pages 14-18, 42-44
___ Joyce	Her roommate	Pages 14-18
___ Ernie	Teen	Pages 14-15
___ Jim Forbes	Father	Pages 18-29, 42-55
___ Desk Sergeant	Policeman	Pages 18-19, 22,
___ Steve Forbes	Jim's brother	Pages 19-20, 23, 46-49
___ Bag Lady	Street character	Pages 20-22
___ Todd Forbes	Jim's son	Pages 26-28, 51-55

___ Woman	Note how she looks	Pages 23-26
___ Maude	Elderly volunteer	Pages 29-33, 35
___ Joshua	Mute paralytic	Pages 29-35
___ Pastor	Old and troubled	Pages 31-35
___ Bill	Dad at picnic	Pages 35-40
___ Chuck	Another dad	Pages 35-41
___ Gloria Forbes	A single mother	Pages 36-41
___ Barbara Forbes	Jim's memory-wife	Pages 49-51, 54-55

AUDITIONER'S NOTES

Roles read   Remarks

_____   _____

_____   _____

_____   _____

_____   _____

_____   _____

Role assigned _____

Father's Day: **SAMPLE SKETCH SCRIPT**
                                   ▽

A FISHY LESSON

Characters: THREE: *two men and one woman*
                 RON: *the Father*
                 VICKI: *a six-year-old daughter*
                 MARK: *Vicki's twin brother*

Tone: Humorous

Running Time: Six minutes

Synopsis: A father is taking his two young children fishing for the first time. From baiting the hook to the first catch, this scene is filled with special moments as the father is forced to teach, to listen, and to answer the difficult questions of life that only children can ask.

Setting/Props: The edge of a dock, or a fishing boat, whatever works best for your imagination. We used three chairs stage center for our set. The Father sat on the back of the center chair, thus giving the impression of being taller than the other two actors. We used adult actors to play the children. The children are holding imaginary fishing poles, intently watching the "water."

RON *(yawning, and closing his eyes, resting):* What a beautiful day for fishing.

VICKI: But we haven't caught any fish, yet.

RON: You know, Vicki, I think you'd have a better chance of catching a fish if you put a worm on your hook.

VICKI: But wouldn't that hurt the worm, Daddy?

RON: I guess you're right, but how else are you going to catch any fish?

VICKI: That's simple. I'll just use my femineminem charm.

RON: Your feminine charm! Vicki, you're only six years old. Where did you ever hear about that?

VICKI: Well, that's how Mommy said she caught you, and you're bigger than these fish.

From *The Lillenas Worship Drama Library, Vol. 6,* by Mike and Colleen Gray. Copyright 1994. Lillenas Publishing Co. Used by permission.

MAKEUP CHART

Production_____

Character _____

Performer _____

Makeup Artist_____

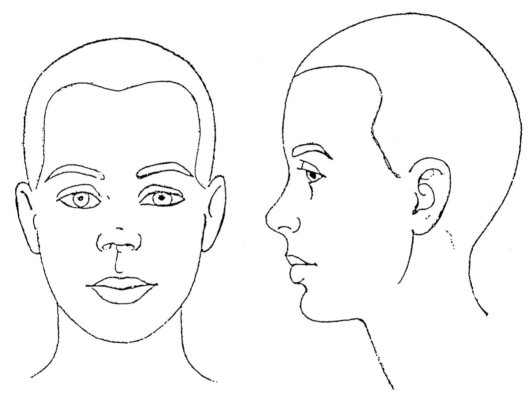

Base _____ Hair _____

Highlights _____ Body _____

Shadow _____ Eye Shadow _____

Lips_____ Pencil _____

Rouge_____

Notes

COSTUME FITTING CHART—MALE

Production:_____ Date: _____ By: _____

Actor:_____ Phone (day): _____

Character: _____ (p.m.) _____

_____

Height:_____ Weight: _____ Waist: _____

Head—Around: _____ Hips: _____ Largest: _____

Head—Ear to Ear: _____ Arm Over (bent): _____

Neck: _____ Arm Under (bent): _____

Neck to Waist: F _____ B _____ Shoulder to Elbow: _____

Underarm to Waist: _____ Bicep:_____

Neck to Floor: _____ Forearm: _____

Underarm to Waist: _____ Shoulder Across: F_____ B _____

Shoulder to Waist: _____ Shoulder Seam: _____

Wrist: _____ Preferred Hand:_____

Chest:_____ Expanded: _____ Thigh: _____

Waist to Knee:_____ Above Knee:_____

Girth: _____ Calf: _____

Inseam:_____ Ankle: _____

Rise: _____ Shoes:_____

Notes: _____

_____

_____

_____

COSTUME FITTING CHART—FEMALE

Production:_____ Date:_____ By:_____

Actress: _____ Phone (day): _____

Character:_____ (p.m.)_____

_____

Height: _____ Weight: _____ Ring: _____ Shoe:_____ Hose:_____

Dress: _____ Skirt: _____ Blouse: _____ Bra: _____ Pants: _____

Dress Measurements   Pants Measurements

Bust: _____   Girth: _____

Bust Below: _____   Thigh:_____

Waist: _____   Knee: _____

Hips:_____   Calf: _____

Front Neck to Waist: _____   Ankle:_____

Back Neck to Waist: _____   Outseam: _____

Cross Back: _____   Inseam:_____

Skirt Length to Knee:_____   Accessories Measurements_____

Skirt Length to Floor:_____   Head: _____

Sleeve: _____   Hat:_____

Armscye: _____   Glove:_____

Neck: _____   Other:

Bicep: _____   _____

Elbow: _____   _____

Wrist: _____   _____

Notes: _____

_____

_____